T0317988

HITLER
HISTORY IN AN HOUR

Also in the *History in an Hour* series

Hitler

History in an Hour

RUPERT COLLEY

**WILLIAM
COLLINS**

William Collins
An imprint of HarperCollins*Publishers* Ltd
77–85 Fulham Palace Road
Hammersmith, London W6 8JB
www.harpercollins.co.uk

Visit the History in an Hour website:
www.historyinanhour.com

Published by William Collins in 2013

First published as an eBook by Harper*Press* in 2011

Copyright © Rupert Colley 2011
Series editor: Rupert Colley
HISTORY IN AN HOUR ® is a registered trademark of
HarperCollins*Publishers* Limited

1

Rupert Colley asserts the moral right to
be identified as the author of this work

A catalogue record for this book
is available from the British Library

ISBN 978-0-00-753913-0

Find out more about HarperCollins and the environment at
www.harpercollins.co.uk/green

Contents

Contents

Introduction

What made a failed Austrian artist into the most reviled and destructive personality of the twentieth century? Where did the seeds of his rabid anti-Semitism lie? How did a marginalized loner become such a moving force in Germany? How could a nation have fallen for such a maverick? What made him so determined to bring about war?

This, in an hour, is the story of Adolf Hitler.

Hitler the Boy

Klara Hitler's life was blighted with tragedy. Her first three children had all died as infants, and when she fell pregnant for a fourth time, the omens were not good. However, this child, born on Easter Saturday, 20 April 1889, although sickly, survived. She named him Adolf.

Adolf Hitler was born in the village of Braunau am Inn, on the Austrian–German border, which Hitler, in the very first sentence of *Mein Kampf*, deemed 'providential' as he was to unite the two countries.

The Hitler family moved several times, always depending on his father Alois's job. Alois's final posting was to a village on the outskirts of Linz where he retired and spent his final years. Adolf, who was five, was to retain a lifelong affection for Linz, which he always regarded as his home town.

Another boy, Edmund, was born in 1894 but lived for less than six years – a devastating blow for the eleven-year-old Hitler. In January 1896 came a daughter, Paula, who survived and lived into adulthood. Klara had had six children but only two survived beyond infancy. But as well as her own two children, Klara looked after her two stepchildren, both from Alois's second marriage. Alois, now in his final years, had no time for his children and preferred to while away his time in the local tavern or looking after his bees. Often drunk, he repeatedly beat Adolf. Klara, who for many years still called her husband 'Uncle', smothered her son but was unable to prevent the thrashings.

Young Hitler did well at primary school but, following the death of his younger brother, less so at secondary where he was frequently criticized for his laziness and arrogance. But he did well at art and harboured ambitions to become an artist. Hitler had no intention of holding down a dreary day job as his father had done all his working life and informed Alois of his artistic aspirations. According to *Mein Kampf*, Hitler Senior reacted with the words, 'Artist? No, never as long as I live.'

But, on 3 January 1903, while enjoying his early-morning glass of wine at the tavern, Alois collapsed and died. Cause of death was either a heart attack or stroke. He was sixty-five; his son thirteen.

Hitler the Youth

Hitler, never enamoured with school, left at sixteen. His mother was disappointed but Adolf had inherited his father's obstinacy and Klara was too soft to assert her authority. Hitler looked back on his years of education with an 'elemental loathing'. Alois had left his family comparatively well off and Hitler, free of his father's bullying and expectations, devoted his efforts to leading a life of idleness. Living in a flat in the centre of Linz, Hitler indulged in his painting by day and his love of the theatre and opera by night. Closeted from the real world by his mother, finding work was never high on Hitler's agenda.

In Linz Hitler made friends with a young man called August Kubizek, or 'Gustl'. They became friends through their shared love of the operas of Richard Wagner, and while Hitler dreamt of becoming a great artist, Kubizek dreamt of becoming a conductor. In the evenings they would dress up and enjoy the opera or the theatre, but during the day, while Kubizek worked at his father's upholstery workshop, Hitler lounged around, daydreaming. Kubizek was the compliant one of the two – while Hitler voiced his opinion on everything, whether good or bad, and sometimes with unnerving passion, Kubizek quietly listened.

Kubizek noted how Hitler fell in love with a girl called Stefanie, but despite his overbearing arrogance in all other matters, he was too painfully self-conscious to try to strike up a conversation with the subject of his affections.

In early 1906, aged sixteen, Hitler visited Vienna for the first time. Staying only two weeks, he returned to Linz, which now seemed small and provincial in comparison. Hitler decided to apply for a place at Vienna's Academy of Fine Arts and, in September 1907, despite his mother's reluctance and aided by a generous loan from his aunt Johanna, he moved to Vienna. Despite passing the initial exams, the would-be artist failed to secure a place. Of the 113 applicants only 28 passed so there was no shame involved but Hitler saw it as a failure and it struck him like a 'bolt from the skies'. His examiners encouraged Hitler to concentrate on architecture instead.

Before Hitler left for Vienna, he and his sister, Paula, had learnt of their mother's breast cancer. Towards the end of 1907, Hitler received word that his mother was dying. He rushed back to Linz and nursed her, devotedly, through her final days. She died on 21 December 1907, aged only forty-seven. According to his mother's Jewish doctor, Edward Bloch, Hitler was with her as she died. 'I have never seen anyone,' wrote Dr Bloch later, 'so prostrate with grief as Adolf Hitler.' Later, Hitler presented the good doctor with one of his paintings. In *Mein Kampf* Hitler wrote of his parents: 'I had honoured my father but loved my mother.' Hitler worshipped his mother and she was perhaps the only person he ever loved. Following her death, Hitler's contact with his family rapidly dwindled.

Hitler returned to Vienna in February 1908, but found that he was missing his only friend, Kubizek. He wrote to Kubizek's father to ask him to allow his son to join him in the city, from where he could pursue his ambition to become a conductor. Kubizek Senior, who hoped that his son would follow him into the upholstery trade, reluctantly gave in. On 22 February, August Kubizek arrived in Vienna to be reunited with his friend.

Kubizek applied for a place at the University of Music and Performing Arts, Vienna and was immediately successful. Kubizek assumed his friend had already started his studies at the Academy of Fine Arts – Hitler had not told anyone of his failure to gain a place. Eventually the truth came out and Hitler, beside himself with rage on telling of his lack of success, blamed everyone but himself.

While Kubizek studied, Hitler slept, daydreamed and conceived grandiose plans that came to nothing. In a fit of enthusiasm he began writing the libretto for an opera along Wagnerian lines, but the enthusiasm soon petered out. In October 1908, Hitler applied a second time for a place at the Academy of Fine Arts and again failed, this time at the initial stage. Again, he kept his failure to himself.

On finishing his first term, Kubizek returned home briefly to Linz. When he came back to Vienna in November 1908 Hitler had moved out. He had left no forwarding address. Kubizek would not see his friend again for another thirty years.

Hitler the Dropout

Suffering bouts of depression and with his aunt's money running out, Hitler moved from one impoverished accommodation to another and spent his last three years in Vienna in a men's hostel. For a while he struck a deal with a fellow guest, Reinhold Hanisch; while Hitler painted Viennese street scenes, Hanisch sold them and the two would split the profit. But while Hanisch managed to sell, Hitler's commitment to painting a picture a day faded and the agreement ended acrimoniously.

Despite having lived in Vienna for six years, Hitler had made few friends, certainly none that he talked about. Acquaintances and ex-room-mates at the hostel remembered him not simply for his anti-Semitism, which was commonplace in Vienna at the turn of the century, but for the extent of his fanaticism against Jews, religion, priests, the Habsburg monarchy, the aristocracy, the middle classes and a number of other pet hates. He preached, with alarming fervour, the cause of a pan-Germany, the unification of all German-speaking people in one state. He would frequent cafés and sermonize to whoever was unfortunate enough to be caught within his orbit. He showed no interest in women, believing that men should remain celibate until the age of twenty-five.

Hitler decided to move to Germany, but had to wait in Vienna until he received his father's small inheritance, which was due on his twenty-fourth birthday – 20 April 1913. Once secured, he was able to leave Vienna and, in May 1913, start afresh in a 'true German city', the city of Munich, the capital of Bavaria, an independent federal state within Germany with its own king, King Ludwig. But Hitler's move to Bavaria was also motivated by the desire to avoid conscription into the Habsburg army. Hitler was not a draft dodger but he despised the Habsburg monarchy so much he had no wish to serve in its army.

His life in Munich differed little from that in Vienna – lacking work, money and friends, living in hovels and wandering aimlessly around the city, admiring the architecture and striking up one-sided conversations in cafés. But Hitler looked back on his time in Munich with fondness, calling it 'by far the happiest time of my life'. In February 1914, the Habsburg army caught up with him and put him in front of a military tribunal in Salzburg, only to declare him unfit for service.

Hitler the Soldier

Six months later, on 1 August 1914, Germany declared war on Russia. The news was received enthusiastically throughout the country and Hitler, especially, was ecstatic.

A photograph taken on 2 August outside the Feldherrenhalle (the Field Marshals' Hall) in Munich shows a large, unruly crowd of happy Germans cheering the news. Amongst them, his face rapt with joy, was the 25-year-old Adolf Hitler.

Hitler tried to enlist immediately, but, as an Austrian, was rejected. A letter to King Ludwig swearing his devotion to the German cause did the trick though, and Hitler was allowed to join the 16th Bavarian Reserve Regiment, known as the List Regiment after its commander, Colonel List.

The List Regiment fought and suffered terribly on the Western Front during the First Battle of Ypres, from October to November 1914. Hitler was awarded the Iron Cross (Second Class) and promoted to the rank of lance corporal for saving a wounded officer stranded in no man's land. 'It was,' he wrote to his Munich landlord, 'the happiest day of my life.' Hitler's task, as a dispatch runner, was to carry messages to and from the headquarters behind the front to the officers in the field, often under artillery fire. Having been promoted to corporal so early on in the war, the expectation would have been promotion to sergeant but his superiors denied him, believing Hitler would never command the respect of his men.

Hitler was not a typical soldier. He did not drink, smoke or seek the company of the local prostitutes, and actively voiced his disgust of these common pursuits. Although respected by his comrades, he seemed uninterested in forming friendships and preferred his own company, reading, sketching, painting watercolours, writing poetry and contemplating. (Hitler's skill as an artist, although far from the genius he sometimes believed he was, was credible, but his poetry left much to be desired.) He received no parcels, nor letters, and when he did talk it was invariably to lecture on one of his pet subjects. His only companion was a white terrier dog he befriended and named Foxl. He was distraught when, on separate occasions, Foxl and his sketchbook were stolen. But the war gave Hitler's life a purpose. The listless, daydreaming wanderer who had never done a day's work had found his vocation.

In October 1916, the List Regiment joined the fray at the Battle of the Somme. Again, the regiment was decimated and Hitler, who had managed to survive unscathed for so long, had become almost a talisman for his comrades. But Hitler's luck was about to run out and on 7 October a piece of shrapnel lodged in his left thigh – or, as later rumoured, his groin, and it was from this incident that the joke that Hitler lacked a testicle came. Despite his protestations that he was fit enough to carry on, Hitler was invalided back to Germany and to Berlin.

It was the future leader's first visit to the capital. While impressed by the city and its architecture and history, Hitler became increasingly angered by the defeatist talk of its impoverished and hungry civilians. He said he saw Jews everywhere, equating them to spiders sucking the blood from people, and the streets were full of workers on strike, whom he despised as cowards and traitors.

In March 1917, much to his delight, Hitler was declared fit and returned to the front. Warmly welcomed by his comrades, Hitler returned to his duties as messenger. He disliked the new recruits who, unlike his optimistic generation, arrived at the front full of pessimism. The regiment fought at Arras and Passchendaele and in August 1918 Hitler was awarded another Iron Cross, this time First Class, a rarity for a non-commissioned officer. The recommendation came from one Hugo Gutmann, an officer in the List Regiment and a Jew.

Two months later, on 13 October 1918, the regiment suffered a gas attack and Hitler and many of his comrades were partly or temporarily blinded. For the second time Hitler was invalided back to Germany, this time to Pomerania. It was during his recuperation that Germany, which not long before had been on the offensive, surrendered and signed the armistice ending the war.

Hitler, still recuperating and fearing for his sight, was devastated.

After stints as a border guard and a prisoner-of-war guard, Hitler returned to Munich in February 1919, totally unsure what the future held for him, and, fearing a return to civilian life, determined to remain in the army.

Hitler the Agitator

Germany, and especially the state of Bavaria, was in chaos during the immediate post-war years. In Berlin a communist coup failed but in Bavaria, on 6 April, a Soviet Republic took over. The 29-year-old Hitler was part of this Soviet Republic, a Bolshevik-inspired regime whose leaders were predominantly Jewish. Hitler was elected as a representative of his battalion to ensure that the army in Munich remained loyal to the Red Republic. In desperation, Germany's chancellor, Friedrich Ebert, called in the Freikorps, a group of violent, far-right ex-soldiers, and the Soviet Republic in Bavaria was brought to a bloody end. Hitler lay low; he played no part in its demise. The Soviet Republic of Bavaria had barely lasted a month but Hitler failed to mention in *Mein Kampf* that for a few weeks at least he served in a communist-inspired, Jewish-led regime.

Following his flirtation with the far left, Hitler remained in the army and started to be groomed as a political instructor, to ensure that the soldiers had not been overly influenced by the communists. In August 1919, encouraged by his mentor, Captain Karl Mayr, he went on a training course and there discovered his talent for public speaking. His speeches were so well attended that he became a star turn. When Mayr was asked, by letter, by a fellow trainee, Adolf Gemlich, to clarify the position on the Jewish question, Mayr passed it on to Hitler for a response. Hitler wrote that Judaism was not a religion but a race and the 'final goal' had to be 'the irrevocable removal of the Jews themselves'. The 'Gemlich letter' is the first-known written statement, at the age of thirty, of Hitler's anti-Semitism. (Captain Mayr was later to renounce Hitler and died in a concentration camp in 1945.)

Hitler monitored political developments in Munich and reported back to his superiors. It was in this role that, on 12 September 1919, Hitler was sent to a meeting of the German Workers' Party, or, to use its German abbreviation, DAP. Founded in January 1919 by a 35-year-old Munich locksmith, Anton Drexler, the DAP was typical of many far-right parties in Germany at the time. It was small and inconsequential, but its membership cards began at the number 500 in order to give the impression of more members. When, during Hitler's visit, one of the DAP's members made a speech in favour of Bavarian independence, Hitler, the great advocate of a pan-Germany, interrupted with an aggressive counter-argument. Drexler was impressed and invited Hitler back to another meeting. He did return and was soon to join the DAP as member 555, not the seventh as he later claimed, and signing his name as *Hittler*. Drexler believed his party could use someone with Hitler's gift of the gab.

In October 1919, Hitler delivered a beer hall speech to an audience of a hundred. Within four months he was attracting over 2,000 listeners with his histrionic, hate-fuelled speeches attacking the enemies of Germany and the scapegoats blamed for all her ills, the Jews, the communists, and the Weimar politicians.

Germany was still in a state of anarchic chaos. In June 1919, the newly formed Weimar government signed the Treaty of Versailles, the document drawn up in Paris by the victorious powers following the war. The treaty stripped Germany of her armed forces, demilitarized the Rhineland (lest France should feel threatened by a military presence on its border), and forced Germany to pay reparations as compensation. But it was the 'war guilt' clause that rankled most with the German population, forced to accept that Germany had been ultimately responsible for the war.

By meekly accepting the treaty, the Weimar government undermined its power from the outset. Extremism flourished amongst the chaos as supporters and thugs of extremist parties, left and right, fought pitched battles in the streets and in the beer halls.

Hitler revelled in the turmoil and offered something different – an unusual blend of nationalism and socialism. In February 1920, having sidelined Drexler, Hitler extended the name of the DAP to reflect its message – the National Socialist German Workers' Party, or NSDAP. Its opponents, in an attempt at derision, soon abbreviated it further to *Nazi*. The newly named party drew up a programme of twenty-five points, its manifesto, which included attacks on the Treaty of Versailles, Jews, advocated a pan-Germany, and called for living space in the east, *Lebensraum*: 'to secure for the German people the land and soil to which they are entitled on this earth'.

In June 1921, Hitler faced the first challenge to his leadership when Drexler and members of the Nazi committee criticized his 'lust for power and personal ambition'. Hitler offered to resign. He knew that without him the party was nothing. The conceited bluff worked and the committee confirmed Hitler as party chairman, and pensioned Drexler off as its 'honorary president'.

Hitler the Revolutionary

The Nazi Party was attracting men who would stay at Hitler's side for many years. Ernst Röhm, a violent, nationalist ex-soldier and ex-member of the Freikorps, was one of Hitler's earliest accomplices, as was the once-dashing First World War fighter pilot, Hermann Göring, who introduced Hitler to the wealthier, more genteel classes. Hitler, always a hater of the aristocracy, pushed his prejudices to one side to play the perfect gentleman, sympathetic to their concerns, and winning much support and financial aid. But at the same time, Hitler maintained his appeal to the working classes as hyperinflation decimated savings overnight and rendered money worthless.

During the early 1920s, Hitler became convinced that the way to power lay in revolution. Revolution had brought power to the Bolsheviks in Russia and had almost done the same for the communists in Germany. Hitler watched with fascination and admiration as Mussolini took power in Italy in October 1922, following his March on Rome. And so in Munich, Hitler planned his overthrow, or putsch, of the Bavarian government followed by a March on Berlin.

Hitler, now aged thirty-four, was invited to a public meeting in a Munich beer hall on the evening of 8 November, hosted by Gustav Ritter von Kahr, leader of the Bavarian government, and the Bavarian chiefs of the police and the army. The opportunity was perfect.

As the meeting progressed, Hitler's armed corps of bodyguards, the Sturmabteilung (the SA), silently surrounded the building. With the bulk of his men in place, others noisily barged into the beer hall, interrupting proceedings and shouting '*Heil Hitler*'. A machine gun was hurled into the room and the audience, fearing a massacre, cowered beneath their chairs. Hitler took his cue, and brandishing a revolver, charged to the front, leapt on to a chair and, firing two shots into the ceiling, declared that he was the new leader of the German government and that the 'National revolution [had] begun'. He then forced the three men on the stage, von Kahr and his chiefs, into a side room, apologizing for the inconvenience.

Returning to the stage, Hitler delivered a rousing speech, winning over his audience who applauded ecstatically. They clapped with equal enthusiasm when Hitler's famous co-conspirator, General Erich von Ludendorff, made his appearance. Ludendorff, as the joint head of Germany's military during the First World War, was well known and well respected, and Hitler hoped that with Ludendorff as his mascot it would win him support. It seemed to be working.

Ludendorff's task was to persuade von Kahr and his chiefs to support the revolution and join the March on Berlin. After some reluctance the three men eventually acquiesced.

Meanwhile, elsewhere in the city, the SA, led by Hitler's confidant, Ernst Röhm, was successfully securing vital strongholds. Hitler, his speech done and his audience converted, left the beer hall to check on progress.

During Hitler's absence, von Kahr and his chiefs confirmed to Ludendorff their new-found allegiance and asked permission to leave so they might issue orders. Ludendorff, always trusting of fellow men in uniforms, gave his approval. Hitler, on his return, was furious that Ludendorff should have been so gullible.

Across the city, scuffles continued and confusion reigned as night turned into day. In the morning, Hitler ordered a march through the city to meet Röhm who, earlier, had seized the offices of the city's War Ministry. With the chastised Ludendorff at his side and about 2,000 men behind him, Hitler set off. But in front of the Field Marshals' Hall in the centre of town their way was blocked by a contingent of police. A gunfight ensued and four police officers and sixteen Nazis were killed. Ludendorff was promptly arrested; Göring, although badly injured, made his escape (eventually to Austria); and Hitler, falling to the ground, dislocated his shoulder.

Hitler managed to escape to a friend's house, where, suicidal, he wrote various letters, including one where he handed over the leadership of the party to Alfred Rosenberg.

Two days later, the police finally caught up with Hitler and arrested him on the charge of high treason.

Hitler the Martyr

Before his trial, languishing in Landesberg Prison in Munich, Hitler fell into a deep depression, talked again of suicide and refused to eat. It was Anton Drexler who eventually persuaded his former protégé to give up the hunger strike.

Opening on 26 February 1924 and lasting thirty-three days, the trial offered Hitler his biggest platform to date. Presiding over the proceedings, the judges were, at heart, Nazi sympathizers. While Ludendorff lied about having anything to do with the putsch and treated the judges as subordinates on the parade ground, Hitler declared his guilt with pride, appealing to the nationalistic patriotism of his listeners: 'I alone bear the responsibility,' he told the bench, 'but I am not a criminal because of that … There is no such thing as treason against the November criminals.'

The court allowed Hitler time to speak at length, delivering not so much a defence but a full political rant. Daily, his words were quoted in full in the following morning's newspapers, making Hitler, hitherto only known in Bavaria, a household name throughout the country.

The nation waited on the verdict. Hitler was found guilty and sentenced to five years. Ludendorff was acquitted. Given his confession, an acquittal for Hitler risked the case going to the higher court where judges made of sterner stuff would not have tolerated Hitler's long speeches and where the maximum penalty for high treason, the death penalty, would have been a distinct possibility. The judge responsible for handing Hitler such a lenient sentence was, on Hitler's appointment as chancellor a decade later, amply rewarded.

The Munich putsch may have failed but Hitler had learnt a useful lesson – that power could not be secured through force but would have to be earned through legitimate means and the ballot box.

Returned to prison, Hitler was spared prison uniform and permitted to wear his lederhosen, granted a spacious room and greeted by the prison warders with a '*Heil Hitler*'. He declined to participate in the obligatory prison sports, saying, 'A leader cannot afford to be beaten at games.'

Although frequently depressed and talking of suicide, Hitler used his time in prison constructively, dictating to Rudolf Hess his autobiographical, ideological rant, *Mein Kampf*. Much of it is devoted to race and the need for a pure race of German Aryans, untainted by the blood of different races. The Aryan race was of the highest order, the 'bearers of culture', the Jewish race (Hitler defined Jews by race not religion) of the lowest. The aim was to eliminate the Jews (referred to throughout the book by various unpleasant metaphors: parasites, germs, vermin) from society. He expanded on many of the themes of the Nazi manifesto, including *Lebensraum*, the union of all German-speaking people, and the treachery of the Treaty of Versailles. *Mein Kampf* sold poorly at first and a 'Second Book', written in 1928, was never published. However, by 1933, with Hitler in power, it outsold all other titles in Germany with the exception of the Bible and made Hitler a very wealthy man.

Hitler served only eight months of his five-year sentence and by the time of his release he had converted most of the prison staff and his fellow prisoners to National Socialism.

Hitler's handing over of power to Rosenberg was a shrewd move. Rosenberg had been a member of the DAP, joining it even before Hitler. At the risk of the party disintegrating, Hitler knew that Rosenberg, lacking the necessary credentials, would make a poor leader and pose no threat to his own authority. Sure enough, on Hitler's release from prison, Rosenberg stepped aside.

Immediately on his release Hitler took up the reins of his party. Visiting the Bavarian president, Dr Held, he promised that from then on the Nazi Party would respect the legal process. The ban placed on the party within the province was lifted, and Held confided to his colleagues that the wild beast had been tamed. Hitler's first public speech since his release, in the same beer hall in Munich where he had tried to overthrow the government, attracted a vast audience and generated much excitement. Hitler was back.

Hitler the Politician

For five years, from 1924, the Weimar Republic enjoyed its golden years. The Dawes Plan, named after its American originator, Charles G. Dawes, produced a financial package that put Germany on the road to recovery. The French left the Ruhr, reparations were reduced to a more manageable level (and eventually dropped altogether), and inflation steadily fell as employment rose.

The Nazi Party itself began to show worrying signs of a rift within its hierarchy. Its more socialist wing, led by the Strasser brothers, Gregor and Otto, had attracted mass support in northern Germany, ably assisted by former communist Josef Goebbels. During a conference in January 1926, from which Hitler was absent, Goebbels called for the removal of Hitler from the party leadership, referring to Hitler in true Bolshevik language as a 'petty bourgeois'.

Hitler had to act. Three weeks later he called a meeting and there asserted his authority. The party was not a democratic party – he, alone, was its leader – and he expected nothing less than unquestioning loyalty from its members. He then reiterated his frequently voiced message that was to have such an appeal to Germans over the coming few years – that he, Hitler, was the saviour of the nation, that he transcended party politics and he alone would restore Germany's pride. He talked of change and revolution while waxing lyrical about preserving Germany's traditional past. It was a message to the party faithful that soon found an audience throughout the country. Gregor Strasser had suggested changes to the Nazi manifesto, a suggestion which Hitler firmly rejected; the 25-point programme was sacrosanct, the 'foundation of our religion'. Sections in the party believed that power had to be won through revolution. But Hitler was firm – there was to be no second beer hall putsch. Power would be achieved through the proper channels.

In Goebbels, Hitler saw not just a potential enemy but a man of great ability and so Hitler went on the charm offensive, eventually winning Goebbels over and offering him the post of the gauleiter (regional leader) of Berlin. The Nazis were faring poorly in the capital but with Goebbels in charge the situation quickly changed.

Germany's periods of depression or prosperity reflected the rise and fall of the Nazis' fortunes. In the national elections of May 1928, the Nazi Party won only twelve seats in the Reichstag. But the Communist Party had done well, and this was enough to give Hitler hope – it showed that the German people had had enough of moderates and the Weimar democracy, and were crying out for radicalism. Hitler equated democracy with weakness; democracy gave everyone a voice, but no one the power.

But then, following the Wall Street Crash of October 1929, the Weimar golden years came to an abrupt end. The US called in its loans, triggering a new bout of high unemployment, poverty and loss of business. With the situation critical, the chancellor, Heinrich

Brüning, was issuing emergency decrees approved not by the Reichstag but President Hindenburg. In the September 1930 elections, before which the Nazis campaigned tirelessly, the party gained 107 seats. As the country fell into ruin, the ascendancy of Hitler began.

The Nazi Party tried every means to block Brüning's emergency decrees, to the point that Hitler was invited to a meeting with the president with a view to finding a degree of accommodation. But Hindenburg was bored and irritated by the preachy Hitler and dismissed him out of hand.

Hindenburg soon had to change his mind. In the Reichstag elections of July 1932, Hitler offered the only alternative to the elderly incumbent and although Hindenburg won, he did so by the narrowest of margins.

Twice, in 1931 and 1932, Hitler was offered a post in the German coalition government. Twice he refused. Hitler was interested in only one post – that of chancellor. It seemed almost possible when, in the elections of July 1932, the Nazi Party won 230 seats in the Reichstag and polled almost 40 per cent of the vote, making it the largest party in Germany.

The new chancellor, Franz von Papen, felt it would be safer to have Hitler in the government where he could be contained, rather than causing mischief from outside. However, the ageing President Hindenburg refused to allow an ex-corporal to be his chancellor. After another round of elections, in November 1932, the Nazis were reduced to 196 seats, despite the slogan 'Hitler, our last hope'. It seemed as if Hitler's star was waning.

Von Papen was then sacked as chancellor and replaced by Kurt von Schleicher, who attempted to form a national coalition. Feeling slighted, von Papen offered Hitler a deal. He suggested a power-sharing partnership with Hitler as chancellor and himself as vice chancellor, but in effect Hitler's equal. Von Papen took the proposal to the president again but promising that, as vice chancellor, he (von Papen) would hold the real power, rendering the Nazi Party inconsequential. 'In two months,' said von Papen, 'we'll have pushed Hitler into a corner where he can squeal to his heart's content.' At first, Hindenburg refused but von Schleicher, having failed to form a coalition, resigned. Thus, Hindenburg accepted von Papen's proposal and on 30 January 1933, Hitler was duly appointed chancellor of a coalition government that contained only three National Socialists. Hitler's moment had come. Von Papen too was delighted and bragged about having 'hired' Hitler.

Hitler the Leader

On coming to power Hitler immediately set to work: curtailing press and political freedom and informing his military chiefs that rearmament and conquest in the east were fundamental to reviving Germany's economy.

Then, four weeks later, on the night of 27 February 1933, came an event that played straight into Hitler's hands – the Reichstag Fire. Hitler saw it as a 'God-given signal'. The culprit, a suspected communist, was 24-year-old Marinus van der Lubbe, an unemployed Dutch bricklayer who, having used his shirt to start the fire, was found half-naked, hiding within the Reichstag.

Although van der Lubbe denied any involvement with the communists, they were, according to Hitler, attempting a putsch. Thousands of known communists were arrested, tortured and either murdered or placed in the newly opened concentration camps for 'protective custody'.

The day after the fire, Hindenburg accepted Hitler's request for a decree suspending all political and civil liberties as a 'temporary' measure for the 'protection of the people and state'.

The exact events causing the fire have never been properly established but it seems unlikely that van der Lubbe, despite his insistence, could have acted alone. Rumours persisted even at the time that the Nazis were implicated, if not the government, then the party. But whatever the circumstances, the fire helped Hitler consolidate his power. The temporary suspension of liberties was never revoked and any active opposition to the Nazis was stifled. When, the following month, the last parliamentary elections took place, only Hitler, it was claimed, could save Germany from the Jews and communists. The SA intimidated all other parties into silence and the Nazis polled 44 per cent of the vote, not enough for a majority but enough to quash any future political resistance. And, on 10 January 1934, three days short of his twenty-fifth birthday, van der Lubbe was beheaded.

In early 1933, Hitler proposed the Enabling Act to allow him to dispense with the constitution and the electoral system. The Nazis bullied any opposition into silence and the Reichstag duly voted in favour and in doing so did away with its own power. The Enabling Act, passed in late March 1933, effectively ditched the constitution altogether. There would be no more elections, nor constitutional safeguards, to keep Hitler in check.

The SA, meanwhile, felt that Hitler had not given them their due reward for helping the Nazis into power. Their loyalties lay not with Hitler, but their leader, Ernst Röhm, and they talked excitedly of a 'second revolution' with Röhm as the leader of the People's Party. Röhm, the only person who called Hitler 'Adolf' and not '*Mein Führer*', saw himself as equal to Hitler. Röhm viewed the army as too traditional and anachronistic, and proposed merging it with the SA under his command.

This alarmed the army and its chief, Werner von Blomberg. Blomberg promised Hitler the support of the army in securing the presidency following the anticipated death of the frail Hindenburg, and in return the army should retain its independence from Röhm.

Pressurized by the army and Hindenburg to act, Hitler had to do something. And he did. On the night of 30 June 1934, the SS, a rival paramilitary organization loyal to Hitler, carried out a purge of the SA and all opponents of Hitler's regime. Men who had crossed Hitler in the past were butchered. Hitler took it upon himself to arrest Röhm personally, marching into his hotel room in Bad Wiessee, where, pointing a revolver, he yelled, 'You're under arrest, you pig.' Röhm was taken to a Munich prison. But Hitler and Röhm had been old comrades and, in a fit of nostalgia, Hitler found it difficult to order his murder. Hitler offered Röhm the chance to kill himself – a revolver was left in his room and he was given ten minutes. When the ten minutes elapsed and no shot had been heard, an SS officer marched in and killed the bare-chested Röhm at point-blank range.

Hitler was praised all round for his assertive actions. Blomberg applauded 'the Führer's soldierly determination and exemplary courage'. Göring, who hated and felt threatened by Röhm, said, 'We all approve, always, what our Führer does.'

A month later, on 2 August, Hindenburg died. Bypassing the niceties of a presidential election, Hitler duly became president without opposition. Blomberg not only kept his word but extended it by obliging his army to swear an oath of allegiance, not to the president, nor the state, but to Hitler himself. Three weeks later Hitler asked the German people, by referendum, whether to combine the posts of president and chancellor. Thirty-eight million people voted in favour – 89.9 per cent.

But Röhm had been right about Blomberg, and after four years

Hitler found the army chief too traditional and too moderate for his liking. In January 1938, Blomberg married a woman thirty-five years his junior, and Hitler and Göring stood as witnesses. When, three weeks later, it transpired she had been a prostitute, Blomberg was forced to resign. Hitler, the former corporal, now took command and became supreme commander of Germany's armed forces.

Hitler the Diplomat

After coming to power Hitler immediately set about ripping apart the Treaty of Versailles. The payment of reparations may have been quietly dropped but the rest of the treaty remained in place. Four days after being appointed chancellor, Hitler spoke of the need for an expanded military force to be in place by 1938 so that Germany would be strong enough to make good his objective of finding living space in eastern Europe. But during these early years of power, Hitler usually hid his real intentions, claiming that Germany only wanted parity with other European powers. Beyond these 'reasonable' demands, further military claims were not on the agenda: 'Germany will of its own accord never break the peace,' Hitler told one British correspondent in 1935.

But Germany's whole economy was geared towards war – a programme of rearmament was implemented, conscription introduced and an air force secretly assembled. In 1936, Göring became plenipotentiary for the Four-Year Plan. With effective control of Hitler's rearmament policy, his task was to reduce Germany's dependency on imports in preparation for war.

Later in 1936, Hitler, in an audacious move and against the advice of his generals, advanced his troops into the Rhineland, an area that had been demilitarized as part of the Treaty of Versailles in order to protect France's eastern border against future German expansion. The gamble paid off – France did nothing, while Britain felt that Germany was merely reclaiming 'her own back yard'. Satisfied, Hitler, whose prestige at home rocketed as a result, re-assured Europe with the words 'We have no more territorial claims to make in Europe.'

In 1938 Germany took over Austria and united the two countries. This *Anchluss* was generally welcomed by the Austrians, except the Austrian Jews who were to pay dearly, and when Hitler visited Linz he was given a rapturous welcome. For Hitler it was a return to the town he always considered home and while there he laid wreaths at the graves of his parents.

Hitler's next objective was to incorporate the 3 million Germans living on the Czech–German border, the Sudetenland, an area of 11,000 square miles, into the Third Reich. The culmination of much diplomatic squabbling was the Munich Agreement, signed in September 1938, that allowed Hitler to have his way on the condition that he made no further territorial demands. Hitler had already told Britain's prime minister, Neville Chamberlain, that the Sudetenland was the 'last major problem to be solved'. Chamberlain returned to Britain pleased that through his negotiation he had secured 'peace for our time'. But just six months later, in March 1939, Hitler invaded the rest of Czechoslovakia.

Next on Hitler's agenda was Poland.

Hitler had signed various treaties since coming to power, each one motivated by pragmatism rather than ideological merit. He signed a ten-year non-aggression pact with Poland (1934), a naval agreement with Britain (1935), aided the far-right nationalists during the Spanish Civil War (1936–1939), withdrew Germany from the League of Nations (1936), signed the Anti-Comintern (anti-communist) Pact with Japan (1936) and the 'Pact of Steel' with Italy (1939). But the most astonishing piece of diplomacy was the signing on 23 August 1939 of a ten-year non-aggression pact with the Soviet Union. It allowed Hitler to further his ambitions, namely the invasion of Poland, without fear of the Soviet Union's interference.

War now seemed inevitable.

Hitler the Warlord

At 4.45 on the morning of Friday, 1 September 1939, the whole weight of Germany's military might fell on Poland. Two days later, Britain and France declared war on Germany. The Second World War had begun.

The war started with a number of spectacular victories for Germany – within two years Hitler had subjugated fourteen nations, including Poland, Denmark, Norway, Belgium, Holland, France, Romania, Yugoslavia and Greece. But it was never enough. Hitler's ideological need for living space in the east drove him to invade the Soviet Union in June 1941. Days before the invasion, Hitler confided to Goebbels: 'Once we have won who is going to question our methods?'

Six months later, following Japan's attack on Pearl Harbor, he declared war on the United States. Despite initial success in Russia, the German advance was stopped within sight of Moscow. The

Russian winter and the unending resources of the Soviet Union began to take its toll on the rapidly depleting German forces.

With the defeat at Stalingrad in February 1943, the downfall of Nazi Germany was only a matter of time. As Russia regained territory lost and started its own counterattack into Germany, the Allies, starting with the Normandy landings in June 1944, attacked from the west.

The Axis was an alliance in name only. Unlike the Allies, the efforts of Germany, Italy and Japan were rarely co-ordinated. Once Hitler had launched the attack on the Soviet Union, a simultaneous attack on Russia's eastern flank by Japan, forcing Stalin into a war on two fronts, would have aided the Germans enormously. But no such proposal, however obvious, was made.

Hitler continually underestimated the opposition. 'You have only to kick in the door,' he said confidently about invading the Soviet Union, 'and the whole rotten structure will come crashing down.' Two tons of Iron Crosses were waiting in Germany for those involved with the capture of Moscow. Hitler believed that the Russian population, embittered by Stalin's harsh rule, would welcome his troops. In many instances they did, but instead of harnessing this allegiance, the Nazis' brutal methods soon alienated these potential collaborators.

As the war turned against Germany, Hitler changed the personnel around him with dizzying frequency, often bringing back into favour those he had previously banished, and thus undermining any consistency. Those who dared stand up to him risked dismissal (although not, as in Stalin's circle, execution) so that ultimately Hitler surrounded himself with sycophants and yes-men, people he could easily control and manipulate. He measured a general's worth not by his ability but by his ideological adherence and preferred generals who brought him good news even if the news lacked any substance.

Only Hitler's opinion counted. While Stalin was prepared to

listen to those brave enough to suggest an opposite point of view as long as he could take the credit, Hitler underestimated the capacity of his ablest generals, rarely listened or heeded advice and preferred to rely on his own intuition rather than hard facts, a strategy that had served him well for most of his political life but that was increasingly at odds with the truth as the war turned against him. Hitler issued numerous 'stand or die' orders, not allowing his troops space to withdraw and thereby giving them no room to counterattack.

On 20 July 1944, Hitler survived an assassination attempt in his 'Wolf's Lair' in East Prussia; the 'July Bomb Plot'. It was perpetrated by Nazi officers led by Count Claus von Stauffenberg, who hoped that with Hitler's death they could shorten the war. Although von Stauffenberg managed to plant and detonate a two-pound bomb, Hitler survived, having suffered only superficial injuries.

Considering Hitler's proximity to the bomb, his survival was miraculous. Hitler himself put his survival down to the hand of providence. Germany, the fates dictated, would win the war and Hitler's life had been spared to ensure it.

Von Stauffenberg and his co-conspirators were rounded up and executed, their deaths recorded on film and sent to the Wolf's Lair for Hitler to watch at his pleasure.

Hitler the Man

Following his release from prison in 1924 Hitler became increasingly aloof. Friendship, which had always been difficult, became impossible. Albert Speer wrote in his memoirs, 'If Hitler had had friends, I would have been his friend.'

Hitler made poor conversation and seemed incapable of listening. From the coffee bars in Vienna to the tables of aristocratic Germany, Hitler liked to hold forth, his conversation degenerating into monologues to the point of ruining a cordial atmosphere, first boring and then embarrassing all those around him. Although his frequent rages were essentially a display of showmanship, he was capable of losing all control of his temper.

Hitler had an amazing memory, especially for technical facts about weaponry, ships and tanks, and could retain the smallest details. And he could be vain. He never allowed his official photographer, Heinrich Hoffmann, to photograph him wearing his spectacles, but such was his long-sightedness that many of his speeches had to be typed in large print. His accent was strongly Austrian, which he did nothing to disguise, believing it added to his distinctive style. His gaze could be intense and, for its recipient, quite unnerving. Those unable to hold his gaze he viewed with suspicion.

Hitler was an avid reader and had a library of over 16,000 books, mainly politics, economics and philosophy, many titles marked with underlining or margin notes. For relaxation he enjoyed American Westerns. He loved opera and adored the works of Wagner, although his favourite piece of music was Franz Lehar's *The Merry Widow*.

Although he later claimed he regretted writing it, *Mein Kampf* made Hitler rich. He bought a large plot of land in Berchtesgaden in the Bavarian Alps and there had his country retreat, the Berghof, built. Fifty existing homes, hotels and a home for disabled children were compulsorily bought, their owners threatened with concentration camps if they dared to object, and six thousand workers, of whom fourteen died, were involved in its construction.

Hitler, who never wore a watch, was a night person, often working through to the small hours. He would get up late, usually around lunchtime, receive his daily dose of stimulants from his personal physician, Dr Theodor Morrell, attend to urgent business then disappear into his private cinema to watch the latest films, including many that had been banned by his regime. He would go to bed in the early hours of the morning.

Hitler was adamantly anti-smoking, and although he drank in the earlier days he later became virtually teetotal. He also avoided tea and coffee, preferring instead herbal infusions, and, following the suicide of his niece in 1931, became a vegetarian. After the seventeenth assassination attempt on his life in July 1944, Hitler became convinced that he risked being poisoned and ordered constant checks on his food, soap and toothpaste.

Hitler had two Alsatians called Blondi, one after the other. The first he had shot when she became elderly and the second he took into the bunker with him. Once, when the second Blondi was ill, Hitler waited anxiously for the daily report on her progress, while, at the same time, absent-mindedly signing death warrants of officers who had shown signs of cowardice or defeatism. Blondi was mated and in early April 1945 bore five puppies, the strongest of whom Hitler named Wolf. Hitler's future wife, Eva, had two dogs and their conversation was often dominated by canine issues. At the end, he tested the newly delivered batch of cyanide capsules on Blondi; she died instantly. The puppies were shot.

Hitler was aware of his mortality: 'I know I shall never reach the ripe old age of the ordinary citizen,' he once said. He saw his existence as preordained and righteous: 'A genius is born only once a century and for that reason I cannot leave the fulfilment of these tasks to my successors.' Hitler firmly believed that his rise to power was no accident and that he had been chosen, not by God, but by providence, for his position. In September 1936 he told a Nazi rally, 'This is the miracle of our times, that you have found me among so many millions. And I have found you; that is Germany's fortune.' He believed that he, the saviour of Germany, had been entrusted to speak on behalf of its people.

Although in 1942 Hitler said, 'I am certainly not a brutal man by nature,' he cared little for the individual – the State was everything, and the individual, even a German, was insignificant. 'If we don't win then even as we go down we will take half the world with us,' he said on the eve of war. While Churchill, whom Hitler once called 'a Jew-besotted, half-American drunkard', made great efforts to visit the victims of German bombs, Hitler never visited his people during their hour of need, not wanting to be associated with failure. Nor did he visit his wounded soldiers for fear of appearing sentimental.

Hitler's Women

Hitler was never truly comfortable in the company of women. His first love, in Linz, was a girl called Stefanie but, lacking the courage, he never spoke to her. Instead he wrote love poems about her which the poor Kubizek had to endure. He extolled the virtues of men remaining celibate until the age of twenty-five. He was repulsed and fascinated by prostitutes, and although he preached that only men of inferior races went to prostitutes, he obliged Kubizek to accompany him on trips into Vienna's red-light districts. Rumours persisted that Hitler caught syphilis from a Jewish prostitute. In the early 1920s, Hitler's driver spoke of them cruising the Munich nightclubs.

Once he had become a national figure, Hitler's relations with women were always marred by his belief that he was wedded to his mission. A wife would not only be a distraction, but could damage his popularity in the eyes of his female followers.

Evidence of this first surfaced during his trial following the failed Munich putsch in which the courtroom was jammed daily with female admirers. On the day of sentencing it was festooned with flowers.

In 1926, the 37-year-old Hitler began seeing a sixteen-year-old called Maria (or 'Mitzi') Reiter. But his dedication to his mission caused her to be sidelined. Depressed by his lack of attention, Reiter tried to commit suicide.

In 1929, Hitler started on a relationship, maybe intimate, with the daughter of his half-sister, twenty-year-old Geli Raubal. Raubal moved into Hitler's Munich flat and Hitler became obsessed by his niece and boiled over in rage when she started dating his driver, who was immediately sacked (although later reinstated). Hitler started controlling every aspect of Raubal's life. On 19 September 1931, she was found dead in Hitler's flat. Aged twenty-three, she had shot herself. Devastated, Hitler became more withdrawn. Heinrich Hoffmann, his official photographer, later stated that Raubal's death 'was when the seeds of inhumanity began to grow inside Hitler'.

Eva Braun worked as a photographic assistant and model for Hoffmann and it was through him she met the forty-year-old Hitler as a seventeen-year-old in 1929. Their relationship began soon after Raubal's suicide, though possibly before. Raubal's jealousy of Braun has been mooted as a possible cause of her suicide. Again, Hitler's lack of attention resulted in an attempted suicide. Twice Braun tried, once by shooting herself, the second time by poison. Although Hitler looked after her materially, Braun was usually marginalized and only Hitler's immediate circle knew of her existence. As the end of the war approached Braun refused to leave Hitler's side and joined him inside the bunker beneath the Reich Chancellery. Finally, aged thirty-three, Braun was allowed to marry her man. Within forty hours they were dead.

Hitler's Health

Following the war, rumours abounded about Hitler's mental and physical health as a way of explaining his actions: his mind had been irreplaceably damaged by a bout of hypnosis that went wrong; his First World War wound had deprived him of a testicle; he had a stunted penis after an altercation with a goat; he had syphilis; he was addicted to cocaine.

What is obvious is that Hitler's health deteriorated rapidly as the war began to turn against Germany. He became increasingly reliant on 'my dear doctor' Theodor Morrell, who fed him on a morning dose of stimulants to the point of dependency and several sleeping pills at night. But Morrell was more of a provider than adviser and whatever his patient demanded he supplied. When other physicians questioned Morrell's methods, Hitler dismissed them as 'fools'.

From mid-1943 visitors who had not seen Hitler for a while

were shocked by his appearance – his hair had turned grey, he had become jaundiced and his skin had lost its colour, his cheeks were sunken and there were heavy bags under his eyes. He walked slowly with a stoop and frequently had to stop to catch his breath; he suffered from flatulence and halitosis, and his left arm shook continuously and hung uselessly at his side, fuelling speculation that Hitler was suffering from the onset of Parkinson's disease. He had to keep an oxygen tank in his bedroom for when he woke up short of breath. He scratched the skin around his neck and ears until they bled.

After years of shouting Hitler twice had to have operations on his vocal cords. He had high-blood pressure and was often doubled up with chronic stomach pains and suffered from the occasional fainting fit. From early April 1945, his right eye caused him pain and Morrell administered daily doses of drops that supposedly included traces of cocaine. His self-imposed incarceration within the bunker, and the total lack of sunlight and fresh air, exacerbated his problems and he looked considerably older than his fifty-five years. But he was still capable of flying into a rage.

Hitler the Anti-Semite

Visions of the evil Jew forcing himself on young Aryan women obsessed Hitler. His morbid hatred of Jews may have originated during his years in Vienna. With a Jewish population of 8.6 per cent, Vienna was rife with anti-Semitism, and Hitler certainly adhered to the ideas of the late-nineteenth-century Viennese politician Georg Ritter von Schönerer. Schönerer, a fanatical anti-Semite, was obsessed by Aryan purity and his 'Away from Rome' party relied heavily on rituals and symbols, while his followers hailed him as their Führer – their leader – all of which was later copied and amplified by the Nazis. Schönerer's influence had waned by the time Hitler had arrived in the city, but his ideas were still being bandied about. In 1897, the new mayor of Vienna, Karl Lueger, was also openly anti-Semitic and an influence on much of the Viennese youth, including the young Hitler.

In Hitler's mind the Jew was responsible for all that was wrong with Germany. The Bolsheviks, another of Hitler's great hates, were mainly Jewish and it was the Jews within the Weimar Republic that had surrendered the war and signed the hateful, dishonourable Treaty of Versailles.

Once in power Hitler pushed through hundreds of anti-Jewish measures. In September 1935, the Nuremberg Race Laws came into effect, legitimizing anti-Semitism as part of the Nazi state. Deemed as 'non-citizens', Jews were denied German citizenship and all political and civil rights.

On the night of 9 November 1938, Goebbels initiated the pogrom that became known as Kristallnacht or the 'Night of Broken Glass'. Synagogues and schools were burnt down; businesses looted and ransacked; thousands of Jews beaten up and nearly a hundred murdered.

Speaking to the Reichstag in January 1939, Hitler was still referring back to the Jewish conspiracy that supposedly defeated Germany at the end of the First World War: 'This day will be avenged,' he said, adding that another world war would result in the 'annihilation of the Jewish race in Europe'.

With the outbreak of war, the Nazis immediately began killing or ghettoizing Jews. Over a million Jews had been shot on the edge of grave pits, but the Nazi hierarchy considered the process too time-consuming and detrimental to the mental health of the murder squads. Seeking alternative methods, the Germans began experimenting with gas, using carbon monoxide in mobile units, but it was considered too slow and inefficient.

Eventually, after experiments on Soviet prisoners of war in Auschwitz during September 1941, Zyklon B gas was introduced into the newly established death camps, capable of murdering vast numbers at a time.

On 20 January 1942, senior Nazis met at Berlin's Lake Wannsee to formalize the 'Final Solution' – the programme to eliminate all Jews – in a two-hour meeting chaired by Reinhard Heydrich.

In 1945, as defeat became inevitable, logic would dictate that all available resources, men and equipment, should have been concentrated in the military effort. But rather than diminishing the programme of extermination, Hitler stepped it up, giving it even greater priority. Time was of the essence and Hitler's ideological destiny took precedence even over winning the war.

In July 1944, Soviet forces liberated the first extermination camps, including Treblinka and, in January 1945, Auschwitz. By the end of the war, six million Jews had been murdered, a third of whom were children. Only one-fifth of Jews in German-occupied Europe, including women and children, survived the war.

Reflecting back on his life, Hitler was critical of what he perceived as his weaknesses or indecisiveness especially in his conduct of the war. But the one thing he looked back proudly on was how he had dealt with the Jews – he had, he said, cleansed 'the German *Lebensraum* of the Jewish poison'.

Hitler the End

In January 1945, as the Soviet army bore down on Germany, Hitler left his headquarters in East Prussia and moved back to Berlin and into the Reich Chancellery. A month later, he went underground into the Chancellery's air-raid shelter, thirty-three feet below ground, a cavern of dimly lit rooms made of high-quality three-metre-thick concrete. With no fresh air and no sign of daylight, its oppressiveness soon began to tell on its occupants.

Shuffling around with a stoop, Hitler looked much older than his fifty-five years. A new pain in his eye required daily doses of cocaine drops, and, perhaps from the onset of Parkinson's disease, his left hand shook constantly. His eyesight had become poor and he needed his documents written in extra-large print, produced on specially made 'Führer typewriters'. His sense of balance had become impaired and he frequently had to sit down or lean on a companion. He ate poorly – mainly devouring large portions of cake. He had fallen out with many of his senior colleagues, in particular Göring and Himmler, both of whom he accused of treachery and ordered to be arrested and court-martialled. Goebbels, however, remained loyal to the last, and continued to broadcast to the nation, demanding ever greater effort and sacrifice against the enemy.

In his final days, Hitler ordered a scorched-earth policy throughout eastern Germany and the destruction of anything that could be of use to the advancing Soviets. Whatever happened to the German citizen, Hitler had no sympathy. They had proved themselves unworthy of him.

From within the bunker, Hitler continued to dictate operations, but his grip on reality had deserted him. He refused to listen to reports of losses and retreats and ordered a constant stream of counterattacks using non-existent troops and refusing troops that did exist the room to retreat.

On 20 April 1945, Hitler's fifty-sixth and final birthday, he inspected a group of twenty Hitler Youth boys lined up in the Chancellery garden. Hitler, with his quivering left hand behind his back, shook hands with each child, muttered a word or two to each and pinched the cheek of the last, the youngest child. He delivered a short speech and thanked them for their bravery before shuffling back into the bunker. It was to be Hitler's last public appearance.

He returned inside to a stilted birthday celebration.

On 22 April, with news that the Russians were in Berlin, Hitler finally knew that the war was lost. 'I cannot command any more,' he cried, 'the war is lost. But if you gentlemen think I am going to leave Berlin you are making a very big mistake. I'd rather blow my brains out.'

In a ten-minute ceremony during the early hours of 29 April, Hitler married his long-term partner, Eva Braun. Goebbels and

Martin Bormann stood as witnesses as the hastily found registrar asked the couple whether they were of pure Aryan descent and free of any hereditary diseases. The reception, as with the birthday party, was brief and awkward.

That night Hitler dictated his political and personal testaments to his secretary and drew up the composition of the government following his death. The admiral, Karl Donitz, was named as his successor, not as Führer but as president, and Goebbels as chancellor. 'Above all,' he dictated, 'I call on the leaders of the nation and their followers to scrupulously observe the racial laws and to mercilessly resist international Jewry, the universal poisoner of all peoples.'

On 29 April, with the Russians barely 300 metres away from the bunker, Hitler made preparations for his death. News came through of Mussolini's execution, and how the bodies of Mussolini and his mistress had been put on public display in Rome, left to hang upside down and were beaten, urinated and spat upon. Hitler was appalled and insisted that his body be burnt. He did not want his corpse to finish up in Soviet hands like an 'exhibit in a cabinet of curiosities'. He ordered in cans of petrol and the testing of the newly arrived batch of cyanide capsules. The chosen victim was Hitler's much loved Alsatian dog, Blondi.

The following day, 30 April, Goebbels tried one last time to convince the Führer to leave Berlin. But Hitler was not to be denied his final, dramatic curtain call.

Near four o'clock, after a round of farewells, Hitler and his wife of two days retired to his study. Hitler wore upon his tunic his Iron Cross (First Class) and his Wounded badge from the First World War. His entourage waited outside with bated breath. A shot was heard. Hitler had shot himself through the right temple. Braun was also dead. She had swallowed the cyanide.

Their bodies, covered in blankets, were carried out into the

Chancellery garden. There, with artillery exploding around them and neighbouring buildings ablaze, Hitler's wishes were honoured – 200 litres of benzene were poured over the corpses and set alight. With the bodies ablaze, the entourage gave a final Hitler salute then returned to the bunker.

The official announcement, the following day, stated that Hitler had 'fallen at his command post in the Reich Chancellery fighting to the last breath against Bolshevism and for Germany'.

Appendix One: Key Players

Hitler's parents: Alois Hitler (1837–1903) and Klara Hitler (1860–1907)

Alois Schicklgruber was the son of Maria Anna Schicklgruber, a 42-year-old unmarried farm hand, but the identity of his father remains uncertain. The two most likely candidates are Johann Georg Hiedler or his brother Johann Nepomuk Hiedler. On Alois's birth certificate the space for the father's name was left blank and the word *illegitimate* scrolled across it. Johann Georg married Alois's mother when the boy was five, thereby becoming his stepfather. But five years later, following his mother's death, the ten-year-old Alois went to live with his uncle, Johann Nepomuk Hiedler.

At the age of thirteen Alois went to work as an apprentice cobbler before joining the Austrian Customs Service at the age of eighteen, an organization that was to remain his employer for the rest of his working life.

Alois changed his name to Hitler, a variant of his stepfather's name, Hiedler, in January 1876. Johann Georg Hiedler had died nineteen years earlier but his name was added to the birth certificate as the father of the 39-year-old Alois. Thus Alois Schicklgruber became Alois Hitler.

Alois married three times, the first time in 1873 to Anna Glassl, fourteen years his senior. But immediately Alois began having a series of affairs, including one with Franziska 'Fanni' Matzelberger, a household servant.

In 1880, Alois and Anna separated and Alois set up home with Fanni, twenty-four years his junior. But, as a Catholic, Alois was not permitted to divorce. Fanni bore him his first child, Alois Junior, out of wedlock. Anna died in 1883 and within a month Alois and Fanni had married. A daughter, Angela, was born two months later. But within a year, in August 1884, Fanni had died of a lung disorder, aged only twenty-three.

Almost immediately following his second wife's death, Alois made his sixteen-year-old household servant, Klara Pölzl, pregnant. Klara was also his cousin (once removed), and Alois had to apply to the church for permission to marry his pregnant relation, twenty-three years his junior.

With the necessary permission, Alois married Klara, his third wife, in January 1885. Four months later, their first child, Gustav, was born. Ida, a second child, was born a year later. In 1887, Klara gave birth to Otto but the child lived for only three days. Further tragedy was soon to follow with the deaths of both Gustav and Ida within weeks of each other.

Six months after the death of her third child, Klara was pregnant again. This child, born on 20 April 1889, lived. They named him Adolf.

Five years later, Edmund was born and then Paula in 1896. But Klara was fated again with the death of Edmund from measles in 1900. He was six. It devastated his older brother who, as a result, began performing poorly at school. Of Klara's six children, only Adolf and Paula survived.

Klara saw little of her husband, whom for many years she called 'Uncle'. Alois, surrounded by the children of his second and third marriages, preferred to while away his time with his bees or with friends at the tavern. Alois died in 1903 and Klara, aged forty-two, was left as a widow.

Klara contracted breast cancer and an operation in early 1907 failed to stop its spread. Adolf, who had recently moved to Vienna, returned home to Linz to nurse his mother during her final weeks. She died on 21 December 1907, aged forty-seven.

Hitler's siblings

Alois Junior (1882–1956). Half-brother from Alois Hitler's second marriage.

Unable to bear his father's bullying, Alois Junior left home at the age of fourteen and never returned. He moved to Dublin, London and, in 1910, to Liverpool where he married an Englishwoman and had a son, William Patrick Hitler. Alois Junior moved back to Germany, alone, in 1914, with the idea that his wife and son should follow him but the First World War broke out and the family remained apart. He married a second time and had a second son, Heinz, who died in 1942 in a Soviet prisoner-of-war camp, fighting for his uncle Hitler, aged twenty-one. Alois Junior died in West Germany, aged seventy-four, in 1956. Throughout his life his contact with his famous half-brother was minimal.

Angela (1883–1949). Half-sister from Alois Hitler's second marriage.

Following their mother's death in August 1884, Alois Junior (aged two) and Angela (aged one) were brought up by their father and his third wife, Klara. Angela married and had three children. Her second child, Angelika, or Geli, was born in 1908. Her husband died in 1910.

In 1928, Angela, accompanied by Geli, became her half-brother's housekeeper. Hitler became besotted by his niece, and the relationship, which may have been sexual, finished with Geli's suicide in 1931. She was twenty-three.

Angela moved to Dresden and married for a second time to a Nazi architect, Martin Hammitzsch who, after the war, committed suicide. Angela lost contact with Hitler until late in the war. She died aged sixty-six in 1949.

Gustav (1885–1887)

First-born child of Alois and Klara (Adolf Hitler's mother). Died of diphtheria aged two and a half.

Ida (1886–1888)

Second child of Alois and Klara. Died of diphtheria aged eighteen months, just one month after the death of Gustav.

Otto (1887)

Lived for only three days.

Adolf (1889–1945)

Edmund (1894–1900)

Died of measles, a month before his sixth birthday.

Paula (1896–1960)

Klara Hitler gave birth to six children between 1885 and 1896 but only Paula and Adolf survived beyond childhood. Paula and Adolf shared their home with Alois Junior and Angela, their half-brother and half-sister. Paula and Adolf were close and she witnessed her brother's frequent beatings by their father.

Although she lost touch with her brother during his years of poverty, they re-established contact and during the 1930s and 1940s occasionally met. Paula spent much of her life, before and after the war, under the name Paula Wolf (or Wolff), a nickname Hitler had used for her during their childhood.

She was said to have resembled her brother. She died in West Germany in 1960, aged sixty-four.

August Kubizek (Gustl) (1888–1956). Hitler's friend.

Kubizek provides the only substantial witness account of Hitler's early years in Linz and Vienna between 1907 and 1912. Born within nine months of each other, they met in their home town of Linz where a shared love of art and music, especially the operas of Richard Wagner, brought them together. They became firm friends to the point Hitler became resentful if Kubizek paid too much attention to anyone else. While Hitler dreamt of being a great artist, Kubizek, or 'Gustl' to Hitler, dreamt of becoming a famous conductor.

In 1912, Hitler moved to Vienna and Kubizek remained in Linz to work as an apprentice for his father's upholstery business which was destined to become his trade. But Hitler somehow managed to persuade Kubizek's father to allow Gustl to join him in Vienna to pursue his musical ambitions.

Thus the two friends were reunited and sharing a room in Vienna. But while Kubizek was successful in his application to the University of Music and Performing Arts, Vienna, Hitler failed twice to get a place at the Vienna Academy of Fine Arts. So ashamed was he of his failure that for a while Hitler managed to keep it hidden from his friend.

In 1908, Kubizek returned to Vienna after a brief visit back to Linz to find Hitler had moved out and had left no forwarding address. He was not to see Hitler again until thirty years later, in 1938.

Kubizek embarked on what promised to be a successful musical career but this was cut short by the outbreak of war in 1914. Following the war he became a council official.

Hitler, the most powerful man in Germany, was paying a visit to his home town of Linz when he agreed to meet up with Kubizek. They met in a hotel lounge and reminisced for an hour. Hitler offered to revive his old friend's musical career but Kubizek, by now fifty, declined. But he did accept Hitler's offer of funding his three sons through music school, and for years to come Hitler would send birthday presents to Kubizek's elderly mother.

Kubizek reminded Hitler of an occasion when, together in Linz, they went to see a performance of Wagner's *Rienzi*. Hitler came out mesmerized, as if in a trance. Hitler gripped Kubizek's hands and 'spoke of a mission that he was one day to receive from our people, in order to guide them out of slavery, to the heights of freedom'. Hitler remembered the occasion well, looked wistfully at his old friend and said, 'It began at that hour ...'

In 1939 and 1940, Hitler invited Kubizek to sit with him at the Bayreuth Festival in Bavaria, an annual celebration of the music of Richard Wagner. The occasions were, according to Kubizek in words reminiscent of Hitler's style, the 'happiest hours of my earthly existence'. Thus their friendship ended where it had begun thirty years before.

In 1951, Kubizek wrote his memoirs, *Adolf Hitler, My Childhood Friend*, where he stated, 'No power on earth could compel me to deny my friendship with Adolf Hitler.'

Eva Braun (1912–1945)

Eva Braun first met Hitler while working as an assistant and model to Hitler's official photographer, Heinrich Hoffmann. It was 1929 and she was seventeen, Hitler forty. But the relationship did not flourish until after the death, by suicide, of Hitler's niece, Geli, two years later. Germany, as a nation, never knew of Braun's existence as Hitler went to great lengths to keep her hidden from view. He was, as he often remarked, primarily wedded to the German people.

Thus the relationship proved difficult for Braun who was devoted to the Führer. Twice she tried to commit suicide, once by shooting herself, the second time by poison. Concerned, Hitler amply provided for her so that, materially, Braun was very comfortable. But still she remained marginalized. She spent much of her time with Hitler in his mountain retreat, the Berghof at Berchtesgaden, but was only reluctantly accepted by the wives of other senior Nazis. When visitors and dignitaries arrived Braun had to make herself scarce.

She had no interest in politics and spent time with her friends or, if alone, reading romantic novels and watching films. Braun liked to wear make-up, smoke and sunbathe nude – all of which Hitler thoroughly disapproved of, though, surprisingly, he lacked the assertiveness to stop it.

In 1944, Braun wrote to Hitler: 'From our first meeting I swore to follow you anywhere even unto death.' True to her word, in 1945 she joined Hitler in the bunker beneath the Reich Chancellery in Berlin, and despite many opportunities to evacuate, remained at his side.

On 29 April 1945, Hitler finally married Braun. Two days later, with the Soviet army only metres away, the couple committed suicide – Eva by biting into a cyanide capsule. She was thirty-three.

Appendix Two: Timeline of Hitler

1889
20 April: Birth of Adolf Hitler.

1903
3 January: Death of Alois Hitler, Hitler's father.

1907
September: Hitler moves to Vienna.
21 December: Death of Klara Hitler, Hitler's mother.

1913
May: Hitler moves to Munich.

1914
August: Outbreak of First World War. Hitler joins Bavarian army.
December: Hitler awarded Iron Cross (Second Class).

1916
7 October: Hitler wounded and invalided back to Berlin.

1917
March: Hitler returns to the front.

1918
August: Hitler awarded Iron Cross (First Class).

13 October: Hitler temporarily blinded in gas attack. Invalided back to Pomerania.
11 November: End of the First World War.

1919
February: Hitler returns to Munich.
April: Hitler works as a political instructor for the Soviet Republic in Bavaria.
August: Hitler attends course on political instruction.
12 September: Hitler attends meeting of DAP (the German Workers' Party).

1920
24 February: The DAP becomes the Nationalist Socialist German Workers' Party, or NSDAP.

1921
29 July: Hitler becomes leader of the NSDAP.

1923
8 November: The Munich putsch, led by Hitler, fails.

1924
1 April: Hitler is sentenced to five years but serves only eight months.

1925
18 July: Hitler's book, *Mein Kampf,* is published.

1932
31 July: Reichstag elections – the Nazis poll almost 40 per cent of the vote.

1933

30 January: Hitler appointed chancellor within a coalition government.

27 February: The Reichstag Fire.

23 March: Passing of the Enabling Act.

1934

30 June: 'Night of the Long Knives'.

2 August: President Hindenburg dies.

1936

7 March: German army enters the Rhineland.

1938

4 February: Hitler appoints himself commander-in-chief of the armed forces.

12 March: German army enters Austria and *Anschluss* is declared.

29 September: Munich Agreement signed.

1 October: German army occupies the Sudetenland.

9 November: Kristallnacht or the 'Night of Broken Glass'.

1939

15 March: German invasion of Czechoslovakia.

23 August: Germany and Soviet Union sign the Non-Aggression Pact.

Second World War

1939

1 September: Germany invades Poland – start of the Second World War.

3 September: Britain and France declare war on Germany.

1940

9 April: Germany invades Denmark and Norway.
10 May: Germany invades Belgium, Holland and Luxembourg.
15 May: Holland surrenders to Germany.
27 May: Belgium surrenders to Germany.
10 June: Capitulation of Norway.
22 June: France signs armistice with Germany.
10 July: Battle of Britain begins.

1941

30 March: German Afrika Korps begins offensive in North Africa.
6 April: Germany invades Yugoslavia and Greece.
17 April: Yugoslav army surrenders to Germany.
22 June: Operation Barbarossa – Germany invades Soviet Union.
11 December: Germany declares war on USA.

1942

22 August: Stalingrad offensive begins.
23 October: Second Battle of El Alamein begins.

1943

2 February: German surrender at Stalingrad.
13 May: Axis forces in North Africa surrender.
13 October: Italy declares war on Germany.

1944

6 June: Operation Overlord – Allied invasion of Normandy.
20 July: Attempted assassination of Hitler.
25 August: Allies liberate Paris.
3 September: Allies liberate Brussels.
23 October: Soviets enter East Prussia.
4 November: Surrender of Axis forces in Greece.

1945

26 January: Soviet forces liberate Auschwitz.

23 April: Soviets enter Berlin.

30 April: Hitler and Eva Braun commit suicide.

7 May: German unconditional surrender in the West.

8 May: German unconditional surrender in the East.

Got Another Hour?

History in an Hour is a series of eBooks to help the reader learn the basic facts of a given subject area. Everything you need to know is presented in a straightforward narrative and in chronological order. No embedded links to divert your attention, nor a daunting book of 600 pages with a 35-page introduction. Just straight in, to the point, sixty minutes, done. Then, having absorbed the basics, you may feel inspired to explore further. Give yourself sixty minutes and see what you can learn…

To find out more visit http://historyinanhour.com or follow us on twitter: http://twitter.com/historyinanhour

1066: History in an Hour by Kaye Jones

Covering the major events of the year 1066, this is a clear account of England's political turmoil during which the country had three different kings and fought three large-scale battles in defence of the kingdom, including the infamous Battle of Hastings.

The Afghan Wars: History in an Hour by Rupert Colley

A comprehensive overview of the wars that have been fought in Afghanistan for almost four decades, including the politics of the Taliban, why Osama Bin Laden was so significant, and why it is still so hard to achieve peace in the country.

The American Civil War: History in an Hour by Kat Smutz

A clear account of the politics and major turning points of the war that split the country in half as the northern and southern states fought over the right to keep slaves, changing American culture forever.

American Slavery: History in an Hour by Kat Smutz

A broad overview of the major events in the history of American slavery, detailing the arrival of the first slaves, the Southern plantations, the Civil War, and the historical and cultural legacy of slavery in the United States.

Ancient Egypt: History in an Hour by Anthony Holmes

A succinct exploration of the historic rise of Egyptian civilisation and its influence on the world, covering Egyptian gods, mummification and burial rituals, and the Pyramids of Giza.

Black History: History in an Hour by Rupert Colley

A clear overview of the long and varied history of African Americans, including everything from slavery, the Civil War and emancipation to the civil rights movement and the Black Panther Party.

The Cold War: History in an Hour by Rupert Colley

A succinct overview of the politics of the non-violent war, from the end of World War II to the collapse of the USSR in 1991, as Russia and America eyed each other with suspicion and hostility.

Dickens: History in an Hour by Kaye Jones

A comprehensive overview of the life of arguably Britain's most successful and beloved writer, including the poverty of his childhood, the evolution of his novels, his tours of Europe and America, and his occasionally scandalous private life.

George Washington: History in an Hour by David B. McCoy

The essential chronicle of George Washington's life, from his middle-class Virginian upbringing to his unanimous election as America's first president, and the prominent role he played in shaping America as we know it today.

The Gunpowder Plot: History in an Hour by Sinead Fitzgibbon

An engaging account of the infamous plot by a group of Catholic traitors, led by Guy Fawkes, to blow up the Houses of Parliament and James I, including details of the motives behind their drastic actions and how the plot came to be discovered.

Henry VIII's Wives: History in an Hour by Julie Wheeler

An inclusive introduction to the six diverse personalities of Henry VIII's wives, the events that led them to their individual fates, and the different impacts they each had on King and country.

JFK: History in an Hour by Sinead Fitzgibbon

A comprehensive insight into the life of America's youngest elected president, assassinated barely one thousand days into his presidency, examining his navigation of the Space Race, his sympathies with the civil rights movement, and the chronic illness that affected him throughout his life.

The Medieval Anarchy: History in an Hour by Kaye Jones

A look at the unprecedented chaos and disorder that followed the death of King Henry I, leading to England's first, and often forgotten, civil war, as well as an overview of the plots and violence that ensued during this nineteen-year bloody conflict.

Nazi Germany: History in an Hour by Rupert Colley

A concise explanation which covers the major events behind the Nazi Party's climb to power, what it was like to live in Nazi Germany, and how Hitler brought the world into war.

The Queen: History in an Hour by Sinead Fitzgibbon

A compelling history of the UK's second-longest-reigning

monarch, covering her 1953 coronation to her Diamond Jubilee in 2012 and examining her long reign, during which the British Empire has transformed.

The Reformation: History in an Hour by Edward A. Gosselin

A concise look at the spread of religious dissidence across Europe in the sixteenth century, including the events that caused people to question the ideas of the established Catholic Church and the resulting wars, migration and disunity.

The Russian Revolution: History in an Hour by Rupert Colley

Covering all the major events in a straightforward overview of the greatest political experiment ever conducted, and how it continues to influence both Eastern and Western politics today.

The Siege of Leningrad: History in an Hour by Rupert Colley

A broad account of one of the longest sieges in history in which over the course of 900 days the city of Leningrad resisted German invasion, contributing to the defeat of the Nazis at the cost of over one million civilian lives.

South Africa: History in an Hour by Anthony Holmes

A fascinating overview of South Africa's history of oppression and racial inequality and how after years of violence and apartheid, Nelson Mandela, the country's first black President, led the country to unite and become the 'Rainbow Nation'.

Stalin: History in an Hour by Rupert Colley

A succinct exploration of Joseph Stalin's long leadership of the Soviet Union, covering his rise to power, his role in the Russian Revolution, and his terrifying regime that directly and negatively affected the lives of so many.

Titanic: History in an Hour by Sinead Fitzgibbon

An account of the catastrophe, including the failures of the White Star Line, the significance of class and the legacy of the disaster in Britain and America.

The Vietnam War: History in an Hour by Neil Smith

A clear account of the key events of the most important Cold War-era conflict, including the circumstances leading up to the Vietnam War, the deadly guerrilla warfare, the fall of Saigon and the backlash of anti-war protests in America.

World War One: History in an Hour by Rupert Colley

A clear overview of the road to war, the major turning points and battles, and the key leaders involved, as well as the lasting impact the Great War had on almost every country in the world.

World War Two: History in an Hour by Rupert Colley

Covering the major events in a broad overview of the politics and violence of the most devastating conflict the world has ever seen, and how it changed the world in unimaginable ways.